FLOOD

⌐ By WILLIAM MATTHEWS

 FLOOD
poems

William Matthews

An Atlantic Monthly Press Book

Little, Brown and Company   Boston/Toronto

FIRST EDITION

Copyright acknowledgements appear on page 72.

LIBRARY OF CONGRESS CATALOGING IN PUBLICATION DATA
Matthews, William, 1942–
  Flood.

  "An Atlantic Monthly Press book."
  I. Title.
PS3563.A855F5   811'.54   81-20833
ISBN 0-316-55078-7   AACR2
ISBN 0-316-55079-5 (pbk.)

ATLANTIC-LITTLE, BROWN BOOKS
ARE PUBLISHED BY
LITTLE, BROWN AND COMPANY
IN ASSOCIATION WITH
THE ATLANTIC MONTHLY PRESS

BP

Designed by Susan Windheim

*Published simultaneously in Canada
by Little, Brown & Company (Canada) Limited*

PRINTED IN THE UNITED STATES OF AMERICA

for Sharon Bryan

CONTENTS

⌇ THREE

ONE

The long path sap sludges up
through an iris, is it new
each spring? And what would
an iris care for novelty?
Urgent in tatters, it wants
to wrest what routine it can
from the ceaseless shifts
of weather, from the scrounge
it feeds on to grow beautiful
and bigger: last week the space
about to be rumpled
by iris petals was only air
through which a rabbit leapt,
a volley of heartbeats hardly
contained by fur, and then the clay-
colored spaniel in pursuit
and the effortless air
rejoining itself whole.

∽ Cows Grazing at Sunrise

What the sun gives us,
the air it passes through aspires
to take back, and the day's long
bidding begins, itself a sort
of heat. Up goes the warm air
and down comes the cold.
In the cows' several bellies the bicker
of use is loud. Their dense heads
spill shadows thirty feet long,
heads that weigh as much as my grown
children, who can crack my heart:
the right tool makes any job
easy. And don't the cows know it,
and the dewy, fermenting grass?
And isn't the past inevitable,
now that we call the little
we remember of it "the past"?

～ HOUSEWORK

How precise it seems, like a dollhouse,
and look: the tiniest socks ever knit
are crumpled on a chair in your bedroom.
And how still, like the air inside a church
or basketball. How you could have lived
your boyhood here is hard to know,

unless the blandishing lilacs
and slant rain stippling the lamplight
sustained you, and the friendship of dogs,
and the secrecy that flourishes in vacant lots.
For who would sleep, like a cat in a drawer,
in this house memory is always dusting,

unless it be you? I'd hear you on the stairs,
an avalanche of sneakers, and then the sift
of your absence and then I'd begin to rub
the house like a lantern until you came back
and grew up to be me, wondering how to sleep
in this lie of memory unless it be made clean.

When it snowed hard, cars failed
at the hairpin turn above the house.
They'd slur off line and drift
to a ditch—or creep back down,
the driver squinting out from a half-
open door, his hindsight glazed
by snow on the rear window
and cold breath on the mirrors.
Soon he'd be at the house to use
the phone and peer a few feet out
the kitchen window at the black
night and insulating snow.
Those were the uphill cars. One night
a clump of them had gathered
at the turn and I'd gone out
to make my usual remark—
something smug about pride disguised
as something about machines and snow—
and to be in a clump myself. Then
over the hillbrow one mile up the road
came two pale headlights and the whine
of a car doing fifty downhill through
four tufted inches of snow atop a thin
sheet of new ice. That shut us up,
and we turned in thrall, like grass
in wind, to watch the car and all

its people die. Their only chance
would be never to brake, but to let
the force of their folly carry them, as if
it were a law of physics, where it would,
and since the hill was straight until
the hairpin turn, they might make it
that far, and so we unclumped fast
from the turn and its scatter of abandoned cars;
and down the hill it came, the accident.
How beautifully shaped it was, like an arrow,
this violent privation and story
I would have, and it was only beginning.
It must have been going seventy when it
somehow insinuated through the cars
we'd got as far away from as we could,
and it left the road where the road left
a straight downhill line. Halfway
down the Morgans' boulder- and stump-
strewn meadow it clanged and yawed,
one door flew open like a wing, and then
it rolled and tossed in the surf of its last
momentum, and there was no noise from it.
The many I'd imagined in the car were only one.
A woman wiped blood from his crushed
face with a Tampax, though he was dead,
and we stood in the field and stuttered.
Back at the turn two collies barked
at the snowplow with its blue light
turning mildly, at the wrecker, at the police
to whom we told our names and what we saw.
So we began to ravel from the stunned
calm single thing we had become
by not dying, and the county cleared

the turn and everyone went home, and, while
the plow dragged up the slick hill the staunch
clank of its chains, the county cleared the field.

∽ ROMAN STONES IN AUGUST

I hate to think how cold they'll be
by winter. That day I could feel, I could
almost see heat sweat into them,
the way honey slathers a comb shut.
And all night, like discharging
batteries, the stones unhoarded
themselves and heat rose, a vast scrap
swept up a chimney, between the tall
stone buildings in the narrow stone streets.
By dawn, when I first thought to scratch
these simple lines on what paper
I could find, the heat was gone and coming
back, one-winged, and I gave myself
up to my body and fell damply asleep.

*One may be a blameless
bachelor, and it is but a
step to Congreve.*

Marianne Moore

When I was eleven and they
were twenty-two, I fell in love
with twins: that's how I thought
of them, in sum, five run-on
syllables, Connie-and-Bonnie.
They were so resolutely given
as a pair—like father-and-
mother—I never thought to prefer one,
warm in her matching bed
like half an English muffin
in a toaster, though Bonnie
was blonde, lithe, walleyed,
angular, and fey. And Connie
was brunette, shiny-eyed, and
shy, as most true flirts
describe themselves, over and over.

And shouldn't love be an exclusive
passion? To fall in love with twins
made me unfaithful in advance?
It made me paralyzed, or I made

it—my love doubled forever
into mathematical heaven—paralysis.
Frocks rhyme and names confuse
and the world is thicker with sad
futures than lost pasts. And I,
who hoarded names like marbles,
how could I say what I knew?
Indeed, how can I say it now?
I knew the two meanings of *cleave*.
I looked into those eyes I loved,
two brown, two blue, and shut my own
(grey) from any light but mine
and walked straight home and kissed
my parents equally and climbed my growing
body's staircase to the very tip of sleep.

AN AIRLINE BREAKFAST

An egg won't roll well
nor a chicken fly far:
they're supposed to be local.
Like regional writing or thin
wines, they don't travel well.
I do. I can pack in ten minutes.
I remember what I love when I'm gone
and I do not and do not forget it.
The older I grow, the better
I love what I can't see:
the stars in the daytime,
the idea of an omelet,
the reasons I love what I love.
It's what I can see I have to nudge
myself to love, so wonderful
is the imagination. Even this wretched
and exhausted breakfast is OK:
an omelet folded in thirds
like a letter, a doughy roll
and some "champagne": sluggard
bubbles half the size of peas.
But the butter's unsalted
and from the air the earth
is always beautiful, what little
I can see of its pocked skin.
Somewhere down there a family

farm is dying: long live
the family farm, the thinning
topsoil, the wheat in full head,
the sow in her ample flesh.
We're better organized than hunger
and almost as profligate.
Across the farmlands a few
of us in a plane are dragging
a shadow-plane, an anchor
that will not grab.

~ BLOCK PARTY

Something's wrong here. The little terrier
is on a string, like a balloon,
and though the rest of him wriggles
winsomely, his bucket-shaped head
is stiff and heraldic, even as he lifts

from the cobbles. He must be the street's
banner, since now the tradesmen are out,
and women (wives with rolling pins,
prostitutes without), and children,
low to the ground like the hens

we'd see if we were in the country instead
of here, jostled by a butcher with a beef-
hued face (aren't fat people jolly?)
and a skittish-fingered tailor, lank,
come to think of it, as one of his needles.

It seems as if someone is about to sing,
and we would move back from him
a little, as if to give him air,
and sway and be rapt. Or he might
weave among us, like amiable water,

so that by being each of us
circulated through, we'd all become

one thing. Though none of us is named
nor moved to sing, so that we mill about
beneath the dwindling dog, and go back in.

⌣ ROSEWOOD, OHIO

Wakeful in my high window,
against which the careless dark
leaned its whole, relaxed weight,
I'd listen to the scritching crickets
break the long nights into units
of patience and fret. That ever-lapsing
pulse, that half-life—what keeps time
so steadily as decay?—
was all my comfort on an August
night. It seemed I never slept,
but prayed all night by memory.
If I could remember against dark
the sunlit land, it would roll
around again at dawn: streambeds
sucked dry by cottonwoods, grackles
spotting the cornstubble like raisins
in dough, detail after detail,
and then something I'd forget
to recall—so that when it didn't
return I wouldn't know, even,
how to name its loss. Soon nights
would be cold: extra blankets,
better radio reception for night games,
little maps of frost forming
at the windows' edges
like a jigsaw puzzle surrounding

its eventual resolution. . . .
The truth is that I slept well
and that I was awake all night.
Time goes one way only but we
go two: we disappear into the past
and into the future at once,
curl up at night to stretch
in the morning, and in between
we drowse in care of our dreams—
their sheltering, flamboyant wings
stretched over us, one in the past
and one in the future—and in care
of whatever slow hum the body
sleeps by when it will not dream
about itself, Rosewood, or anywhere.

⌁ OUR STRANGE AND
LOVABLE WEATHER

for Daniel Halpern

First frost, and on the windows snow
is visible in embryo,
though Seattle has only one
snow a winter. Mostly we have
cool rain in fog, in drizzle, in mist
and sometimes in fat, candid drops
that lubricate our long, slow springs.
But I'm way ahead of myself.
From behind windows one season
is another. You have to go
out to feel if this is winter
gathering or giving itself up,
though whichever it may be, soon
enough turmoil under leafmold
begins, and the bulbs swell, and up
the longings of themselves spring's first
flowers shinny. February.
Here you can fill in the bad jokes
about weather and change, about
mixed feelings, about time, about
not wanting to die, and by the time
you've run round their circumference
the year has turned to May, and night
drags its feet home slow and dusty
as a schoolboy. But soon it's June,

usually rainy here, then summer
arrives in earnest, as we say,
with its long, flat light pulling
like an anchor against the sun.
How can the year have gone so fast?
Already the cool nights tuned
so perfectly to deep sleep admit
a few slivers of cold, then swatches,
and then they meet and are patterns.
First frost once again, we think.
Time to clear the clog of wet leaves
from the gutters, time to turn off
the water to the outside faucets.
And time to think how what we know
about our lives from watching this
is true enough to live them by,
though anyplace lies about its weather,
just as we lie about our childhoods,
and for the same reason: we can't
say surely what we've undergone,
and need to know, and need to know.

⟿ DESCRIPTIVE PASSAGES

Your hair is drunk again,
someone explains to me.
And it's not only my hair:
no matter how rack-natty
my clothes were, they're rum-
pled on my body, dressed up
like a child performing
for its parents' guests.
How much of childhood
is spent on tiptoe! Clean up,
wise up, speak up, wake up
and act your age. But also one
is uppity: something's gone
to his head, a bubble
in the bloodstream, a scratch
in the record, a bad habit.

No theory can explain
personality, which expands
to include, if it can, all
its contradictory urges.
It's so hard to think about
this fact that we don't:
we use crude code. *The one*
with the limp, with big tits,
with the drunk hair. And we love

so much to be loved—
or failing that, remembered—
that we limp a little, and thrust
out our chests. On me it looks
good, as the hunchback said.

Use description carefully.
For example, today as I
glower out at morning fog
I can feel the fatigue
of matter, how glum a job
endurance is. The gulls
over Lake Union look heavy
and disconsolate, like office life.
Is this all there is, I could ask,
secretly excited
because if it is I've saved
myself so much response
and responsibility.

It's harder than we think
to name our children, but how
can we be accurate?
They'll find stories to live by.
I envision my children
sitting loosely in middle age.
I give them good wine to talk by,
I've lit them a fire if it's cold.
I can't leave them alone, I think
from the grave: a father's work
is never done. One son turns
to the other and says, *You know
how I always think of him?*

I remember his drunk hair.
There's a pause. It's harder
than we think to name
our emotions. *There were those*
sentimental poems he wrote
about us, and his drunk hair,
the other son says, proud
for the intimate talk and sad
for how little such talk says,
though it wasn't drunk that often.

∽ FUNERAL HOMES

So this is what's become of the idea
of purgatory, these long drawers
like card catalogues, as if the after-
life were a neglected scholarship.

Here every clue is false.
Funerals don't happen "at home,"
though death does, since the body
is home. And the houses,

solid as banks but adamantly
residential, imply that we can
take it with us, the shimmer
of matter we inhabit for a while,

or at least can leave it for safe-
keeping with substantial folks
who don't go out much, drink
on their ample porch, or burn lights

late, though nobody sleeps in such houses,
unless the night watchman cheats.
Better he read the classics all night
and think what a dead language means.

⁓ GOOD COMPANY

At dinner we discuss marriage.
Three men, three women (one couple
among us), all six of us wary.
"I use it to frighten myself."
Our true subject is loneliness.
We've been divorced 1.5 times
per heart. "The trick the last half
of our lives is to get our work done."
The golfer we saw from the car
this afternoon, his angered
face in bloom with blood, lashed
his strict ball for going where he'd hit it.
We watched him turn from a worse shot
yet and give us a look like our own,
and on we dawdled through
the afternoon toward dinner,
here. Here means the married
couple's house, of course.
The rest of us use so much time
being alone we don't entertain much.
The wind loops and subsides.
"What a fine night to sleep!"
Upstairs a book falls off a shelf.
We'll be sitting here ages hence:
the scent of lawns, good company, Sancerre,
fitful breezes suddenly earnest.

"What sense does marriage make now?
Both people want jobs, the sad
pleasures of travel, and also
want homes. They don't want dark houses
or to live with cats. They have lives
waiting up for them at home.
Take me, I must read half-an-hour
of Horace before I can sleep."
The conversation luffs. The last
bottle of wine was probably too much
but God we're happy here.
"My husband stopped the papers
and flea-bathed the dog
before he left." One of us has a friend
whose analyst died in mid-session,
non-directive to the end.
Now we're drifting off to our nine lives
and more. Melodramatic wind,
bright moon, dishes to do, a last
little puddle of brandy or not,
and the cars amble home:
the door, the stairs, the sheets
aglow with reticence and moonlight,
and the bed full to its blank brim
with the violent poise of dreams.

TWO

THE WATERS

for James Tate

If you stare out over the waters
on a bright day when the wind is down
and the waters move only to groom
themselves, turning their beautiful faces
a little to guess how the light looks
on them this way, and that. . . .

If you hear them, contented as they seem
to be, and quiet, so that they seethe,
like a slow fire, and their long syllable
is not broken into music. . . .

And if you should carry them with you
like the memory of impossible errands
and not know what you carry, nor how,
so that you feel inelevably mute,
as if from birth, then you will be apt
for speech, for books, and you'll be glib

though it torment you, and you'll rise
to the sacraments of memory and lie down
unable to forget what you can't name,
and the wine in your glass will be ink.

⌒ FLOOD PEAK

Over the rising waters,
like the silver of breath
on a mirror, the shadow
of a cloud luffs by.
This is the way it looks—
beautiful—from far away.

Closer, everything stinks
of the speed it's being ruined,
exploded, rot with a fever.
Doubtless the graves are open
below us and the roads go
everywhere at once.

The water is herding us
upstairs because the house
is swelling like a grain of rice.
We watch a bloated sow
float by, her teats like buttons
the water will undo from inside.

The window over the bed
doesn't rattle anymore,
its frame is so thick with sog.
We said we'd never sleep here
again and now there's nowhere else.

⌒ RECORD FLOOD

Rain pumped snakes from their holes
and rain was so much rain it began
to leak up and bear on its back

the froth of rain that came
to cover the rain that came before.
Rain with rain on its back goes

where its load needs to go,
all the way to brack, fatigue
from going, the surface always

falling into whatever it covers
until it is gone and the new land
looks as though it always looked

like this, no pod-like propane
tanks blooming against cliffs,
no road the old only know

where it was, no bodies waiting
for dental records, no big time.
Only the blue acres drenched by light.

ᵔᶜ TAKEN AT THE FLOOD

Suddenly the drizzle lifts
its dank voice: a slant
rain and then sleet
sizzles at the windows
like a fury so pure it's
dispersed by recognizing it,
one of those cramps you get
by loving your children wrongly
that only wrong love and all
your fatal habits will see
you through, though you
rant against them:
lordly as the froth
on the lip of the waterfall,
you urge them to carry you
over, and they do.

⌣ FLOOD LIGHT

Walking the prairies—sky so vast
and horizon so far around it seems
to fall away from you—

you sense the flood, drained
millennia ago. Here and there the earth
is cracked and scaled, reptilian.

And here and there, as the long light
pours down, you think how the rising
waters would bear up the prairie wind

and its ceaseless murmurs, how silent
this floor would be if the flood
should come again in water.

⌁ FLOOD TIME

Strange to think what solvents
we carry to work and back,
or even on the dull miracles
of commercial flight, and through
O'Hare among the composed
blank faces of the all-day
travelers not squandering
their attentions here, where
there's so little to love and all
of it scratched and marred,
like the faces we love because they
are not strange. And strange to think,
as Braniff launches one of its blue
boomerangs to Dallas and back,
how seldom we use some
of those solvents but carry them
anywhere, like an army, in case,
in case. . . . Should one of us need
suddenly to weep, he might start
(if he wept seldom) like a car
on a cold morning, but soon
weeping is its own event
and the body like a rented hall,
and all too soon the party's
over. I'd better clean this mess,
he thinks. It's like defrosting

the old fridge from boyhood,
all that blurred fur of ice
turns cloudy water, gets thrown
away. The details pool and then
they're not details, they're
experience. Gone is the sound
of a fireplace one day: the seethe
of green wood first and then
suddenly the flames flapping
like hot cloth. Gone is the smell
of that one overripe Pont-l'Évêque: hay
steeped in cow urine, and gone
the speed of the barn settling
around him as a child, and the
blue dark before dawn, the thick
shifting cows, the itch of a new
flannel shirt and the delirium
of being up among huge, warm
shapes when he should be asleep.
But it's gone, along with the path
to get to or from it, along with how
to remember between times
the exact pressure of her head
on his shoulder; it's been washed
away and that's why he wept
who feels lightened now,
though someone else is weeping
near Gate E5, and the other
solvents (it's almost that we serve
them, we who are not anonymous)
we bear on our inexplicable
missions slosh gently inside
us, ready when we are.

∾ FLOOD CLUTTER

By what it has abandoned here
in this topmost splurge of swash,
and in the next one down and then
the next and next, we can see how
the flood, like rage descending its ladder,
disgorged to the air all it had eaten
but its turbid aftermath and self.
Who'd call this pool of clutter flood?

As to how it rose with nothing to climb
but itself, like rhetoric or lust,
what clues we can find here are false,
like the menus we could make by cutting
a shark open: a Louisiana license
plate, a runt tuna, a flashlight. . . .

⌐ UNRELENTING FLOOD

Black key. White key. No,
that's wrong. It's all tactile;
it's not the information
of each struck key we love,
but how the mind and leavened
heart travel by information.
Think how blind and near-
blind pianists range along
their keyboards by clambering
over notes a sighted man
would notice to leave out,
by stringing it all on one
longing, the way bee-fingered,
blind, mountainous Art
Tatum did, the way we like
joy to arrive: in such
unrelenting flood the only
way we can describe it
is by music or another
beautiful abstraction,
like the ray of sunlight
in a child's drawing
running straight to a pig's ear,
tethering us all to our star.

⌒ FLOOD PLAIN

You could pick one up, any one
from the scrupulous profusion
by which accident has sown them here,
smoother from their streambed tenure
than jagged from being strewn, and what

would you say you held? You could draw
one of them, or write the letters for *stone*
in some language, any one of them,
and what then could you say you held?
It would be a clear day, I would be with you,

and we would have a water-lathed box
full of the true history of itself,
to which the history of any treaty
is but a heart-broken footnote.
Only water can read such a book,

or write one. Think how long we've
agreed to love each other, and forgot
to care for that dwindling future, as if
we had the time the stones have, or the time
water takes to redistribute the stones.

～ *EVERYWHERE*

By the way its every
event is local and exact,
and by the reluctance of water
to rise and the way it climbs
its reluctance, so shall you know
flood, and by the way it compiles

the erasure of its parts
and takes to itself the local
until all but sky is water.
On this huge page no breath
will write. The text is already
there, restless, revising itself.

THREE

∽ SAD STORIES

Once upon a time, a story might begin,
hoping to embody two virtues:
it would be unique and it would be
repeatable. To the writer, the story
is only unique: it is his before it can be
anyone else's. But if he told it again,
he'd tell it differently, better.
To the reader, it is only repeatable:
the words never change. And the reader
is helplessly unique, bombarded
by time. The prim book will never be
better, nor will it change, nor will it long
to be anything other than itself, so
it could be said to be happy, perhaps,
even if it is abandoned under a wrought
iron bench by a homely girl in overalls
ashamed to have huge breasts so young.
Over the parched lawn she carries herself
like a bowl of ludicrous damp fruit,
her face so full of the intensity of being
her face, right now, that it's wholly opaque—
its depths, its "inner meanings," as bad
readers would say, have risen so fully
to the surface that they *are* the surface,
and so she knows why she is happy

and therefore beautiful, should someone
be lucky enough to ask: "I'm happy
because I've been reading sad stories."

∿ BURGLARY

for Dave Smith

The family will hate most
the way privacy itself
seems to have been stolen,
and ease and deepest sleep.
What *is* that noise? An owl
threshing the mouse-fluff
from its talons, a spot of blood
like a castemark above its beak.
A dog loping aslant across
the yard. Something that slurs
in the wall. Membranes,
the locked windows pass things
through both ways. The neighbors
sleep less well, and one shuns
her cellar for a week, with its smell
like a packet of ripped-open yeast
and its spoils a family wanted
to own and nobody wants to steal.
Another neighbor sits down to write,
needing to know the name
of something he can't say
without a name, the way
when we first wake we look
a little blurred and shapeless,
and by shaking off those waters
become unique and familiar

to ourselves again, inhabitants
of our names. The man writing
stops for a minute. He doesn't
yet have the name, but a better
reason to need it. He continues
to write. That's why writers
call it "working." From above
the neighborhood looks brighter tonight
than usual. Some of these lights,
as burglars would know, burn
to fool burglars. A light burns
where a man is writing.
One cellar light's been on
for a week by now, though we
can't see it from up here nor know
how we know it's burning.

⌣ SCHOOL FIGURES

for Susan

It's best to work before dawn:
fresh ice, its surface silvered
and opaque, and you scritch out
onto the milky ice, not avid
for grammar, too sleepy for speech.
It's not that you're marking time;
you're melting it grainy under
your runners. Each time you sweep

in your half-sleep around the figure
    eight, your blades are duller
and record how far you've slid
from your margin of error, zero.
That's why you skate it backwards.
It's where you've been you have to go
again, alert enough to numb
every muscle memory but one.

So much learning is forgetting
the many mistakes for the few
lines clear of the flourishes
you thought were style, but were
only personality, indelible as
it seemed. Who but you could

forge those stern exclusions? Where
the line of concentration crosses

itself, cutting and tying its knot
both, there learning and forgetting
are one attention, and are the thrall
that pulls you stiff-ankled over
the ice before dawn, turning
over your shoulder as if you could
skate back into your first
path and get it right for once.

⌐ AVERTED EYES

Imagine the day they found
Wardell Gray dead in a field
in Nevada, broken neck, OD,
mysterious circumstances,
33 and another man
in the tenor chair for Benny
Carter's band that night,
working from charts.
Above the dead musician—
they've not found him yet—
clouds improvise, some
gathering and others frazzling
to wisps as irreversibly
as perfume disperses.
How meekly accidents obey
natural law. By now the sun
is at full parch and the men
sent by the sheriff waver
in the candid heat. Soon
one will find Gray's body,
which I can't describe
because I've looked away,
and probably you would, too.

Instead I'll imagine a balm
of sun: peaches and languorous

bees, Sunday in the south
of France and the delusion
that light and heat resemble desire.
They resemble themselves and
desire matter, something to work on—

which is what we lack
who think loss the source of work:
the beloved dead, our rueful
marriages, our grammar by which
the present is only cadet
to the past. From which we cannot
turn while Wardell Gray's
blurring body gets found and then
assumed into memory's oniony
heaven, far from the opportune earth.

Pissing off the Back of the Boat into the Nivernais Canal

It's so cold my cock is furled
like a nutmeat and cold,
for all its warm aspirations
and traffic of urine. 37
years old and it takes me a second
to find it, the poor pink slug,
so far from the brash volunteer
of the boudoir. I arc a few
finishing stutters into the water.
Already they're converted,
opaque and chill. How com-
modious the dark universe is,
and companionable the stars.
How drunk I am. I shake
my shriveled nozzle and three
drops lurk out like syllables
from before there were languages. Snug
in my pants it will leak a whole sentence
in Latin. How like a lock-keeper's
life a penis biography would be,
bucolic and dull. What the penis
knows of sex is only arithmetic.
The tongue can kiss and tell.
But the imagination has,

as usual, most of the fun.
It makes discriminations,
bad jokes. It knows itself
to be tragic and thereby silly.
And it can tell a dull story well,
drop by reluctant drop.
What it can't do is be a body
nor survive time's acid work
on the body it enlivens,
I think as I try not to pitch
my wine-dulled body and wary
imagination with it into the inky
canal by the small force
of tugging my zipper up.
How much damage to themselves
the body and imagination
can absorb, I think as I drizzle
to sleep, and how much
the imagination makes
of its body of work
a place to recover itself.

⟿ THE BASILICA AT VÉZELAY

for Mary Feeney

On the central spandrel, at
Christ's right shoulder, hovers
a shy, winged calf, holding
a Bible like an autograph-
seeker approaching an author.
Likewise we tourists go in,
as if history were a celebrity.
And how oddly modern and severe
it looks, all stone and stone-colors,
all space and light, as if light
were modern and the dark ages dark.
So it surprises us to learn
from our brochures all this was painted
when built. Maybe garish, even.

The capitals are allegorical—
in this one God's love grinds
the flour of the New
Testament from the wheat of the Old.
My brochure calls this mystic.
I call that kind of thought
"lying down in a blizzard
of imprecision to sleep."
The stone miller and his stone
assistant were carved by a patience
like their own, daily, the slow

and only path to the future,
after men the sculptor knew.
Today's model for the miller
might be driving a taxiful
of Belgians to Châtel Sensoir.
He likes meeting people, but
he's troubled by his daughter,
so smart but so glum, a cloud
in her whirling skirts. If we knew
how to look for it we could see time
passing through him, like blood.

What "mystic" means in the brochure
is that our ignorance is comfortable
to name and the past easy
to imagine. The basilica is 393
feet long. Imagine that. This kind
of vestibule, called a narthex,
is peculiar to Burgundian churches.
Imagine that. What I don't know
and never will makes me weep easily
for human limitation, especially
my own. In 1130 fire slaked itself
on whatever they had here and they
built this in slow revenge. Imagine
1130: the cold town high on the hill
for military reasons, the few foods
and short life-spans. Harder still
to imagine their gaiety, or the good
nights they ate well and long.

The taxi driver's coming back.
"I don't know what to think,"

he thinks. I think of that calf—
legs folded up since he'll never
need them, a sweet grassy daze
in his bas-relief eye, and surely
a wild, erotic terror to hang so near
the gaunt shoulder of Christ,
as close to God as he can bear or get.
I go out into the tiny square.
A boy on a moped is torturing
a beagle with a crumpled ear.
"It's the first day of autumn,"
the waiter at the café says
to nobody in particular,
maybe to autumn. How much does
a calf weigh, I wonder, a stone
calf beautiful and dumb
as a hummingbird? Is art long?
I order a glass of *vin du pays*.
Is life short? I can imagine that.

∽ THE PENALTY FOR BIGAMY
   IS TWO WIVES

I don't understand how Janis Joplin did it, how she
made her voice break out like that in hives of feeling.
I have a friend who writes poems who says he really
wants to be a rock star—the high-heeled boots, the
hand-held mike, the glare of underpants in the front
row, the whole package. He says he likes the way
music throws you back into your body, like organic
food or heroin. But when he sings it is sleek and
abstract except for the pain, like the silhouette of
a dog baying at the moon, almost liver-shaped, a
bell hung from a rope of its own pure yearning.
Naturally his life is exciting, but sometimes I think
he can't tell the difference between salvation and
death. When I listen to my Janis Joplin records I
think of him. Once I got drunk & sloppy and told
him I feared artists always had more fun and more
death, too, and how I had these strong feelings but
nothing to do with them and he said *Don't worry I'd
trade my onion collection for a good cry, wouldn't you?*
I didn't really understand but poetry is how you feel
so I lie back and listen to Janis's dead voice run up
and down my body like a fire that has learned to live
on itself and I think *Here it comes, Grief's beautiful
blow job.* I think about the painter who was said to
paint with his penis and I imagine one of his portraits

letting down a local rain of hair around his penis now too stiff to paint with, as if her diligent silence meant to say *You loved me enough to make me, when will I see you next?* Janis, I don't care what anybody thinks or writes, I don't care if my friend who writes poems is a beautiful fake, like a planetarium ceiling, I want to hold my life in my arms as easily as my body will hold forever the silence for which the mouth slowly opens.

⌒ A LATE MOVIE

On Haiti two years ago he stalled
to a coma and his wife learned
a little voodoo to lure him out.
Since then he's noticed nothing strange
in her except those usual opacities
a husband or wife flies through:
clouds, the weather of others.

Meanwhile she's been burning dried
spiders, etc., and when he discovers her
silly paraphernalia he's happy
to be adamant. Maybe he's seen
something odd in her after all
and is glad to think this is it.

But it wasn't just duff he made her
throw away, nor only the litter
on which decay lies down its bed-
burning body, it was a system
of details, and so a sort of memory.

Whatever it was she's sick without it
and wherever they fall his feet are wrong
and sound to him like heartbeats.
He can hear the space between them grow
and then he can see it, a sift

in which the dwindle and swell
of matter shine, the way salt glowed
in the oceans he dreamed as a boy,
as if the stars were underwater.

His wife's fevers flurry and subside.
She might as well be underwater.
He tries to hold her. His arms waver
and bend. Not that he believes her magic
now, but that his is little but burning
ashes, burning water, burning smoke.
Love might ask anything of you.
Or fire might ask anything of you
and say that its name is love.

∽ BMP BMP

for James McGarrell

Lugubriously enough they're playing
Yes We Have No Bananas at deadpan
half-tempo, and Bechet's beginning
to climb like a fakir's snake,
as if that boulevard-broad vibrato
of his could claim space in the air,
out of the low register. Here comes
a spurious growl from the trombone,
and here comes a flutter of tourist
barrelhouse from the pianist's left hand.
Life is fun when you're good at something
good. Soon they'll do the *Tin Roof Blues*
and use their 246 years
of habit and convention hard.
Now they're headed out and everyone
stops to let Bechet inveigle his way
through eight bars unaccompanied
and then they'll doo dah doo dah doo
bmp bmp. Bechet's in mid-surge as usual
by his first note, which he holds, wobbles
and then pinches off to a staccato spat
with the melody. For a moment this stupid,
lumpy and cynically composed little money-
magnet of a song is played poor and bare
as it is, then he begins to urge it out
from itself. First a shimmering gulp

from the tubular waters of the soprano sax,
in Bechet's mouth the most metallic
woodwind and the most fluid, and then
with that dank air and airborne tone
he punches three quarter-notes
that don't appear in the song but should.
From the last of them he seems to droop,
the way in World War II movies
planes leaving the decks of aircraft carriers
would dip off the lip, then catch the right
resistance from wet air and strain up,
except he's playing against the regular disasters
of the melody his love for flight and flight's
need for gravity. And then he's up, loop
and slur and spiral, and a long, drifting note
at the top, from which, like a child decided
to come home before he's called, he begins to drift
back down, insouciant and exact, and ambles
in the door of the joyous and tacky chorus
just on time for the band to leave together,
headed for the *Tin Roof Blues*.

Too Cold to Snow

Probably because time's so short
(what poem might not begin like that?),
we come to recognize stories so smoothed
by the currents of belief they're no
longer stories: jazz putts up the river
like a tugboat, Abner Doubleday
invents baseball, we always hurt
the ones we love. And it's too cold
to snow tonight in Terre Haute
or Noblesville or Bean Blossom,
much less at either of earth's poles—
which is why those stark, vast
caps are esplanades of sand
but the camels there are frozen.

Even when it's too snowy to be cold
I take long thoughtful walks
with the mysteries for company:
the space people, the unbroken
gossip of the stars, who the first
person was to eat a lobster,
how ambition causes cancer.
And I might find a frozen
leaf in the shape of Atlantis,
if I knew for sure what shape
that was, same as the birthmark

on the back of my true love's knee,
in the fold, if only I'd met
my true love yet, or, if I have
already, if only I'd known it then.

∽ Nabokov's Death

The solid shimmer of his prose
made English lucky that he wrote

plain English butterflies
and guns could read,

if they were fervent readers.
He loved desire. *Ada* could be

pronounced *Ah, Da!* — one
of those interlingual puns

he left, like goofy love notes,
throughout the startled house.

And yet we'll hold to our grief,
stern against grace, because we love

a broken heart, "the little madman
in his padded cell," as Nabokov

once described a fetus. For grief
is a species of prestige, if we mourn

the great, and a kind of power,
as if we had invented what we love

because it completes us. But
our love isn't acid: things deliquesce

on their own. How well he knew that,
who loved the art that reveals art

and all its shabby magic. The duelists
crumple their papier-mâché pistols.

The stage dead rise from the dead.
The world of loss is replete.

⌢ EPITAPHS

Rest lightly on these bones, we urge the earth.
Here lies . . . Here sleeps . . . A blanket of new snow,
we say, as if to tuck the dead under,
Ma in her kerchief and I in my cap,

sleepy after a long day of rubbing
tombstones—a form of printing and erasure,
both. And don't the dead go before us, scouts,
and follow us, like consequence? *Oh yes*

is the answer to that question, a gasp
that would itself make a fine epitaph.
Where there's multiple choice you should believe
your first impulse, and ours, dear dead people,

Ma's and mine: to be proud of you, then
rinsed of pride by the downpour of the dead.

∼ DISTANT CHIRPING BIRDS

for W. S. Merwin

Someone is crumpling beautiful paper.
Noise of a fire clearing its throat,
as if matter were evanescent phlegm.
But the birds sound more dire

and beautiful even than that.
They sound like the first music
composed for icicles, or they sound
like life in another language,

another physics, another desire.
And a strange memory: not words
but what we use words to remember:
something we could almost sing.

ON THE PORCH AT THE FROST PLACE, FRANCONIA, NH

for Stanley Plumly

So here the great man stood,
fermenting malice and poems
we have to be nearly as fierce
against ourselves as he
not to misread by their disguises.
Blue in dawn haze, the tamarack
across the road is new since Frost
and thirty feet tall already.
No doubt he liked to scorch off
morning fog by simply staring through it
long enough so that what he saw
grew visible. "Watching the dragon
come out of the Notch," his children
used to call it. And no wonder
he chose a climate whose winter
and house whose isolation could be
stern enough to his wrath and pity
as to make them seem survival skills
he'd learned on the job, farming
fifty acres of pasture and woods.
For cash crops he had sweat and doubt
and moralizing rage, those staples
of the barter system. And these swift
and aching summers, like the blackberries
I've been poaching down the road

from the house where no one's home—
acid at first and each little globe
of the berry too taut and distinct
from the others, then they swell to hold
the riot of their juices and briefly
the fat berries are perfected to my taste,
and then they begin to leak and blob
and under their crescendo of sugar
I can taste how they make it through winter. . . .
By the time I'm back from a last,
six-berry raid, it's almost dusk,
and more and more mosquitoes
will race around my ear their tiny engines,
the speedboats of the insect world.
I won't be longer on the porch
than it takes to look out once
and see what I've taught myself
in two months here to discern:
night restoring its opacities,
though for an instant as intense
and evanescent as waking from a dream
of eating blackberries and almost
being able to remember it, I think
I see the parts—haze, dusk, light
broken into grains, fatigue,
the mineral dark of the White Mountains,
the wavering shadows steadying themselves—
separate, then joined, then seamless:
the way, in fact, Frost's great poems,
like all great poems, conceal
what they merely know, to be
predicaments. However long
it took to watch what I thought

I saw, it was dark when I was done,
everywhere and on the porch,
and since nothing stopped
my sight, I let it go.

NOTES

"Descriptive Passages": "'After all,' sighed Narcissus the hunchback, 'on *me* it looks good.'" W. H. Auden, *The Dyer's Hand*.

The Flood poems were first published in a limited edition conceived and made by the papermaker Kathryn H. Clark, lithographic printer David Keister, draftsman James McGarrell, printer and graphic designer Wesley B. Tanner, and the poet. A proof edition of six copies was pulled in Bloomington, Indiana, in January 1981; that part of the project was financed by the Bloomington Arts Council, the Ford Foundation, the Indiana University Department of Fine Arts, the Indiana University Foundation, and the National Endowment for the Arts.

"A Late Movie": The poem takes liberties with the plot of the British film *Burn, Witch, Burn* (1962).

"Bmp, Bmp": The poem describes a cadenza Bechet takes on "Tin Roof Blues" on his *Back to Memphis* album with Sammy Price, recorded in 1956 (Jazz Legacy #51, 1978).

Some of these poems first appeared in the following magazines.

American Poetry Review: "Descriptive Passages," "Good Company," "Unrelenting Flood"

Antaeus: "An Airline Breakfast," "Burglary," "Cows Grazing at Sunrise," "Funeral Homes," "Nabokov's Death," "Roman Stones in August," "School Figures"

The Atlantic Monthly: "The Waters," "New," "On the Porch at the Frost Place, Franconia, NH"

Blue Buildings: "Epitaphs"

Cornell Review: "Record Flood"

Durak: "A Late Movie"

Georgia Review: "Flood Time"

Karamu: "Taken at the Flood"

New England Review: "Bmp, Bmp," "Flood Clutter," "Rosewood, Ohio"

New Virginia Review: "The Basilica at Vézelay"

The New Yorker: "Housework"

Ohio Review: "Averted Eyes," "The Penalty for Bigamy Is Two Wives"

Pequod: "Flood Light," "Unsated Flood"

Plainsong: "Distant Chirping Birds"

Ploughshares: "Bystanders"

Seattle Review: "Pissing off the Back of the Boat into the Nivernais Canal," "Sad Stories," "Too Cold to Snow"

Sonora Review: "Twins"

Tendril: "Flood Plain"

Vanderbilt Review: "Flood Peak"

Vegetable Box: "Block Party"

Thanks to the trustees of the Frost Place (Franconia, New Hampshire) and to the John Simon Guggenheim Memorial Foundation for aid and comfort during the writing of these poems.